Uncommon Civics: The Teaching Handbook for Activating Citizenship

Diego Iván Durán-Medina, M.A., M.Ed.

ISBN: 1725734419
ISBN-13: 978-1725734418

DEDICATION

I dedicate this book to every teacher who inspired me, and to the students who taught me precious lessons in courage and resilience.

I dedicate this book to my mother, Dr. Carmen Durán-Medina, who instilled in me the value of hard work, education and pursuing dreams as an educator and immigrant. My mom taught me the value of community service and a relentless pursuit of justice with intelligence and love.

I am also grateful to my brother, mentor and friend, José De Jesús, who believed in my vision long before I did, and who helped me realize it.

CONTENTS

ACKNOWLEDGMENTS

I am grateful to all the people who read, edited and commented on this manuscript. A special thank you to Rachel for being a great colleague and editor, your suggestions made me a better writer and this a better book. A special debt of gratitude to Raffi and Heather, two talented and brilliant graphic designers who helped design the book cover and Uncommon Civics logo. Thank you for believing in this work and helping craft my vision.

I must also recognize the impact that four places have had on my development as a servant leader, an intellectual and a volunteer: New York City, a place where I learned how to think, the value of resilience and how to survive; Pine Ridge Reservation, South Dakota, the place where I learned silence, forgiveness and how to witness; Washington, D.C., where I grew up and began my service-learning career as a teenager in Montgomery County, Maryland; and finally, New Orleans, a city that always gives me exactly what I need and the place where the idea of Uncommon Civics was born.

I am not from any of these cities, but I am *of them*.

1
TRADITIONAL VS. UNCOMMON CIVICS

To be uncommon is to be remarkable, exceptional and unusual.

Uncommon Civics strives to be unique and groundbreaking as a new concept and model for teaching citizenship skills by placing students at the center of their learning and is markedly different from what has come before. Uncommon Civics moves from outdated notions of civics taught as some combination of facts and history to a curriculum that can shape a whole new kind of society for our country and the world. Uncommon Civics is about a new civic future.

There are deep problems with how civics and citizenship are traditionally taught. A new conversation and methodology is needed. This book also aims to bridge crucial gaps in civic engagement. There is a gap between what students learn and know and how they can apply this knowledge in their lived reality. There is a more nuanced assumption that might exist with educators that to have academic knowledge is the same as to have civic intelligence; that is, the power and skills to know how to turn ideas, ideals and values into reality and positive change. Perhaps the most dangerous gap this book addresses is what happens when heroes and heroines become so perfect and sanctimonious that they become unreachable, and therefore, unteachable. Students have no idea how to make history. They learn as though living in a museum; they can read about those who have changed the world, but rarely are they taught as though they have already been chosen to become historical figures and destined for lives of meaning through service.

This book assumes that all students have opinions and values that drive a desire to improve the world, and it further assumes that with support from educators, they can realize the change they seek.

The teaching of civics is inextricably tied to the meaning and context of civics, so it becomes vital to critically examine civics education. This process begins by posing problems associated with the teaching of civics so that educators can understand the critical need for a new approach through the Uncommon Civics model.

First, a clarification of what Uncommon Civics is not. It is not simply how a bill becomes a law, or what state laws exist to govern or encourage certain behavior or random historical facts tied to one's place of origin or residence. It is also not merely the study of patriotic symbols, rituals, customs or rites of passage.

These concepts might be important but only in terms of one central question: How is it that citizens learn how to change society?

And by asking how citizens change society, a relevant secondary question emerges: What knowledge and skills are essential to the work of improving society through activating citizenship?

Schools are one of the primary institutions for teaching the above mentioned citizenship skills, so one last important question should be addressed: What are different ways that schools can and should teach in order to develop citizenship skills in students?

When civics becomes reduced to simplistic formulas of society, and how government "should" be, it creates a problematic distortion of reality for students. This is perhaps why students both may come to hate social studies courses with its rote memorization along with an increasing and urgent sense that what is taught has very little applicability to reality. Because it does not speak to their lives and lived experiences, civics can quickly be discounted as uninteresting and unimportant. This is dangerous for both schools and democracy.

Uncommon Civics offers a model for guiding students on their journeys to becoming better citizens through a different learning process. It begins with placing the student at the center of learning.

Take, for example, how a bill becomes a law. Does anyone reading this chapter honestly think that a student could walk into Congress or any other legislative body and understand lawmaking without also understanding all of the infinite nuances that go into getting a bill passed? What of the various constituencies and how they have influenced the process? What about lobbying and special interests?

This example leads to perhaps a more pressing question: Why should the student care unless the bill being discussed has some direct bearing on their lives? We have failed students when the material discussed in class cannot explain what is happening in the news. It is also why fascinating history is often sterilized with random, meaningless facts that students memorize for an exam and quickly forget. There is no narrative about how those dates and facts tie back to current reality. This is called the problem of congruence.

The second problem posed by present day teaching of civics is around impact. When civics is posed as a concept that happens "to others"-people like lawmakers, voters, lobbyists and lawyers hidden away in legislative chambers or in Congress and Washington, DC, there can be a dangerous disassociation with students not realizing that they are also impacted by these laws. National legislation almost always has some sort of local impact. Students must understand this.

One does not all of a sudden begin being a citizen at 18. If students do not understand how laws and civic engagement govern their behavior, opportunities and outlook for their own lived realities, it makes sense they would feel little to no agency in learning about those laws and little motivation to learn about and change conditions that could better their lives or improve their communities.

This also speaks to the problem of focusing strictly on voting, which will be expanded on later in this work. While voting is of primary importance, citizenship does not magically begin on the first day a ballot or vote is submitted. Citizenship is a fundamental right and responsibility that should be taught and developed from the first day of school. Students should not have to wait to begin becoming citizens-it is part of knowing how to be human and part of society. Hence, there is a problem of delayed gratification around citizenship.

There also exists a neutrality problem. This is where civics/history/social studies are taught as topics that have winners and losers, with the victors controlling the narrative, and yet, there is an assumption that the curricula used and opinions within the texts are free of bias and/or values. History is presented as neutral, and in doing so, there is little space or time to discuss other perspectives and challenging grand narratives. To be clear: it is not the job of educators to push certain political beliefs on students. However, educators should teach students how to critically think about social studies as matters of debate, discourse, discussion and disagreement.

A responsibility exists to be honest and forthcoming to students about how the beliefs and values of educators affect the teaching models, methods and materials used. Pretending like educators are all neutral delivery machines emptying content into innocent, empty spaces within the head of our students is misguided at best and disingenuous at its worst. Students deserve better.

Instead, educators can embrace a new framework where the responsibility of posing questions around values and creating spaces for our students to explore, define and critique beliefs is embraced and expanded upon. The problem of perceived neutrality is turned into a learning opportunity when students are asked to discern the values hidden or evident within a text or lesson. This also allows for students to think of other perspectives and how values may shift depending on the view. Finally, students can think about their own personal values and how it affects how they read a text or situation.

After all, do faculty not work at certain schools because of the values they teach? Do educators not choose certain texts and omit others because they align or run counter to certain values and beliefs? Why shy away from the teaching and discussions of values in classrooms and schools? Instead, educators can serve as models for how to form worldviews based on rational thought and a focus on critical analysis, a process good for both democracies and schools.

Finally, and most formidably, is the problem of agency for civics. Often, students never have an opportunity to apply their learning. Civics is not just laws nor simply a culture around citizenship or patriotism, it must also be about application and action. Civics must also be about arming students with actual tools, methods and skills that can be used to develop voice around real issues for agency. What is meant by Uncommon Civics is this: a teaching model that helps students have an understanding of themselves, the issues they care about and a command of mediums to deliver powerful messages to the world. All activism begins with agency and powerful messaging.

The five problems of congruence, impact, delayed gratification, neutrality and agency often hinder the effective teaching and learning of civics. Uncommon Civics provides a way forward.

The Uncommon Civics class can transform classrooms into living laboratories for democracy by helping students develop as scholars and citizens. Through understanding themselves as citizens and researching topics as scholars, they can be uncommon in their power.

Uncommon Civics teaches the present while preparing students to shape a better future around their ideals, values and opinions. A student practicing activated citizenship grows through reflection, analysis and engagement. In doing so, students can change society for the better. Through their actions, activated citizens help embody and strengthen democratic ideals of life, liberty, and pursuit of happiness. Young citizens serve as living reminders that lofty principles must be put into practice to have actual relevance and meaning. Uncommon Civics can change the citizenry, and in doing so, change the country.

The book is strategically organized for educators and administrators, especially for those in charge of curriculum. The book is designed such that it could be read over a weekend and put into practice on Monday. For those looking to implement a classroom course or augment already existing courses, chapter 3-6 will provide a syllabus, template for the class and sample lessons. For educators looking to understand, clarify and deepen civic engagement on a more systemic level, chapters 7 and 8 provide a solid foundation.

The first two chapters begin to setup problems that deserve attention in order to improve the developing of citizens and strengthening democracy: Chapter 1 focuses on challenges posed by the teaching of civics and Chapter 2 offers insights into expanding the understanding of civic engagement to be more broad and holistic.

Chapters 3-6 outline the Uncommon Civics class. Uncommon Civics exists as an academic course developed over a decade, primarily within independent schools. The class serves as a course on developing students as change agents. The course can be adapted to work for public schools, whether in a traditional classroom setting or in after school and/or summer programs. The class allows for students to focus on one issue which can be expanded upon through multiple civic engagement initiatives outlined in the next chapter.

Chapter 7 focuses on the field of civic engagement and serves as a guide on naming multiple approaches and methods to activating citizenship.

Chapter 8 outlines the universe of the person in charge of implementing civic engagement. An argument is made for elevating this work so that it exists in every single school across the world.

The conclusion serves as a call to action to reflect on what the future holds for teaching and learning civic engagement through the story of one very special student.

2
THE 4V MODEL OF CIVIC ENGAGEMENT

In discussing Uncommon Civics, it is important to define citizenship as an active rather than passive process. One can be granted certain rights and responsibilities upon birth or legal status and one can speak of status based on law, paperwork and genealogy.

The process of shaping citizens, especially in classrooms, is quite different. Uncommon Civics focuses on "becoming" a citizen, which is learning a certain set of skills for developing voice that validate and enhance a democratic society. This activated citizenship asks more of the citizen and must be earned. By extension, it assumes that schools, both public and private, and other community institutions are responsible for the crucial, important and difficult work of developing citizens. That means that all educators, especially those working in the social sciences and teaching social studies, have a special responsibility to think about what it means to develop citizens. Citizenship is not just a title, it is a learning process, and as such, can be analyzed, developed and improved upon.

When you think of good citizenship skills, what comes to mind? Most people tend to focus on voting and volunteering.

Yet there is more to citizenship than a ballot or a service hour. The 4V model is a useful template for pushing and broadening the concept of citizenship. Citizenship can be expanded to include two new terms: values and voice. It is worthwhile to discuss each in detail and explore their relationship to what is taught in schools with the aim of developing better citizens through Uncommon Civics.

Values exist all around society, and they drive both personal and professional inclinations. Values shape much of what humans think about and accomplish. They help govern institutions. Candidates for office are often judged on their values. Movements are shaped around values. Schools have statements about what is valued as an institution and what values students should expect to learn. Values serve as important guiding lights; they serve as a compass for living.

Yet what is almost never done is asking students to think about their own values. What is it that they believe in and why? Where did these values come from? Which ones are theirs and which ones have been given to them? Which ones can students justify to themselves and others? Which ones matter the most? What are the values that guide their life and purpose? Which values guide their service?

These questions matter when deciding to take young people seriously. Within the classroom, this means caring enough to ask these questions and providing the space, time and support to listen and help them develop answers. What would a class look like that asks these kinds of questions? How does one use the answers to these questions to move young people to become more engaged and civically intelligent? These questions will be addressed in more detail in the next chapter after exploring the rest of the Vs.

Because of the role that volunteers have played in both democracy and social movements, volunteering is an obvious part of the 4Vs. For Uncommon Civics, volunteering must be done with great care, forethought, planning and reflection. It is volunteering for two purposes: the first, to truly help and never do harm, and the second, to learn. This means that students who choose to volunteer do so with questions that they want to answer in mind. They actively seek context and knowledge so they can better understand an issue or a topic, and therefore help address the root cause(s). In this way, volunteering is both a physical and an intellectual endeavor. In completing their service, the student can say with some confidence that they have grappled with the topic at hand both inside and outside the classroom walls. This is what is meant by service-learning.

On to voting. For many students who are years away from turning 18, voting will remain an abstract concept that although important, will not be practiced until the end of their education or until they have left the institutions. This is perhaps one of the most urgent and important questions for educators thinking about civics education.

Preparing students to be future voters is of utmost importance, but it cannot be the sole definition of good citizenship. Not only does delayed gratification come into play as mentioned in Chapter 1, there are too many nuances that might affect voting; are the issues that the student cares about even on the ballot? Are there politicians who reflect views that speak to the student? Will they be around to benefit from, assess and critique the proposed policies being voted on? What ties them to the outcomes of their choices in voting?

Voting is an act that occurs in a continuum. Students still require a space where they can research issues, platforms and candidates so they know what and who to vote for. Students also need ways to influence those in power and hold them accountable after elections.

Voting is always important and necessary within a democracy and yet, it is necessary to broaden our understanding of citizenship through allowing students to research issues while learning new skills.

Uncommon Civics begins with the internal: defining, uncovering and shaping values and opinions so that it can be followed by action, whether through an eventual ballot, service or other means of social change. What connects the internal development with the external action is a deep and sustained reflection on values combined with the development of voice. This allows students to not only learn about citizenship in theory, but to actually have the means for which to practice it. This is a process that does not need to wait until age 18.

As the fourth and final V in the 4V model, voice is the most important skill and outcome in activating citizenship through Uncommon Civics. Voice means helping students think about, reflect, craft and deliver a message that is based on combining the head and the heart. Focusing on voice means having students define what they value, listening to multiple perspectives on their topics and crafting a powerful statement that inspires others to reflect and act. Additionally, the support of caring adults and peers and the ability to defend their beliefs are central to the development of student voice.

The Uncommon Civics course addresses crucial civic gaps and amplifies the 4Vs through a set of learning goals, reading materials, activities and a proven process for organizing and sequencing the learning for students. It is a course that is meant to be learned and lived, focusing on what is important to students, following a rigorous intellectual inquiry process while harnessing the power of art and creativity in order to powerfully communicate values through voice.

3

THE UNCOMMON CIVICS CLASS

Ideally, every school should offer the Uncommon Civics class. Every young person should have an opportunity to develop their thinking and speak their truth so that communities can be strengthened by the energy, wisdom and power of young people.

For civics, educators are tasked with designing learning experiences that provide answers, but more importantly, establish frameworks for questioning. Educators understand deeply the power of a question; how it can open new trails of learning, or turn a boring subject or topic into an interesting pursuit of knowledge by asking the right question, in the right way, at the right time. This also applies to citizenship and the training of citizens. In a time where students have information within their pocket with an internet connection, one should question the value of teaching a random set of facts, histories and laws and the thinking that it qualifies as adequate civics training. Even after circumstances change based on election outcomes and different administrations govern, essential questions around the rights and responsibilities of citizenship still remain.

New generations of citizens require both teachers and students to ask fundamental questions about concepts that are considered founding principles. And yet they mean little if the mindset needed to understand those principles is not taught. The principles are meaningless if the skills needed to put ideals into practice are not developed or practiced. A democracy is only as strong as the lessons taught to maintain it along with constant practice by its citizens.

This chapter contains the lessons and activities used to help develop and activate citizenship within young people at the high school level.

Class Description from the Uncommon Civics syllabus:

Becoming an activated citizen begins with knowing the values we want to live by. This, in turn, helps us define causes we believe in. By knowing ourselves, we are able to clearly communicate our values clearly and powerfully so others may be inspired to join our cause. All social change begins with a central, clear and powerful message.

In this class, you will (1) define what you believe and value through activities, readings and reflection and critically examine what civic engagement means through readings, discussions and texts, (2) research an issue that you are passionate about and (3) craft a clear message using art and technology to reach and teach others.

In this class, your political orientation is not as important as your ability and willingness to engage with ideas, especially those ideas that are new and quite possibly in opposition to what you already believe. An open mind is necessary. The class is essentially about what it means to be an engaged citizen along with reflection on your rights and responsibilities as a citizen.

The class involves three main components:

1. (Heart) Values: What do you believe in and why? What do others believe in and how have they acted on those beliefs?
2. (Impart) Blueprint: Research and reflection process involving factual analysis, discernment of what is true and can be supported by evidence from multiple credible sources.
3. (Art) Artifact: A message with a medium based on the finished blueprint: How will you get your voice heard?

This class has mostly been taught as a semester class, usually with 12-13 weeks of class time and 5-6 hours per week, totaling roughly 70-80 contact hours. I usually assess students on four key areas with each section worth 25%: (1) reflection on readings with five written reflections, each worth 5%, (2) blueprint research, (3) creation of an artifact and (4) quality of contributions to class discussions. The class can be adapted as needed as long as the three main components exist.

Course texts used for readings and graded written responses:

Soul of A Citizen: Living With Conviction In Challenging Times by Paul Rogat Loeb

Healing the Heart of Democracy: The Courage To Create a Politics Worthy of the Human Spirit by Parker Palmer

The Impossible Will Take a Little While: Perseverance and Hope in Troubled Times by Paul Rogat Loeb

What Kind of Citizen? Educating Our Children for the Common Good by Joel Westheimer

You're More Powerful than You Think: A Citizen's Guide to Making Change Happen by Eric Liu

The Civically Engaged Reader: A Diverse Collection of Short Provocative Readings on Civic Activity by Adam Davis (Author) and Elizabeth Lynn (Editor)

Signs of Resistance: A Visual History of Protest in America by Bonnie Siegler

Make Art Not War: Political Protest Posters from the Twentieth Century by Ralph Young

Desiderata by Max Ehrmann

On Civil Disobedience by Henry David Thoreau

Enduring understanding for the course:

An engaged citizen knows what they believe in and is able to communicate their values through effective messaging using skills in art and technology.

The class has three sections: **Values (Heart), Blueprint (Impart) and Artifact (Art).**

Learning Target #1: Heart/Values
Self: **You will be able to name your guiding values.**
Others: **You will critically assess opinions/values on democracy, citizenship and civic engagement.**

This learning target focuses on values exercises and readings from the books listed in the previous page, always asking:

What values drive the author? What have I learned about my own values through reflecting on the values of others?

Learning Target #2: Impart/Blueprint
Research: You will use the blueprint process in order to critically analyze your chosen topic.

This target introduces the blueprint process along with identifying and critiquing sources, recognizing bias and forming informed opinions, especially by listening to contrasting views.

Learning Target #3: Art/Artifact
Message: You will create an artifact that combines your values, research and message through an artistic medium to deliver a powerful message to your intended audience.

This target introduces multiple mediums as artifact options: theater, spoken word, comic books/graphic novels, speeches, monologues, photography, short films, including fiction and/or documentaries, posters, songs, podcasts, murals/street art, pamphlets and poetry. This list is can be expanded as needed.

Over the next three chapters, each component for the Uncommon Civics course is outlined in detail.

4
VALUES: THE HEART OF THE MATTER

Exploring the values held by students is an important first step in the Uncommon Civics class. For many students, this might be the first time in their educational career where they have the space, time and opportunity to think deeply about what it is that they value and why. It also might be the first time an adult has asked what they think about social issues and cared enough to listen to their response.

The first part of the Uncommon Civics is the process of identifying the values students bring to the class and distilling where their values come from and which ones they want to "own." Young people have all heard messages from society, the media, their communities and their families on what they should believe. There is a general expectation that students will bring different beliefs and worldviews to the course, and the class is made stronger by multiple, different and contrasting perspectives. Part of the course includes challenging beliefs and values, especially through the blueprint and the assigned reflections from texts on civics and citizenship.

The class begins with asking fundamental questions about the students and the course: What values should drive our course and guide how we speak to each other and spend time together? Where do you come from and what moves you? What do you believe in and why? What do you stand for? What issues are you willing to stand up for? What talents do you already possess to help you develop voice?

1. Norms for Our Class
(20-30 minutes)

Question for reflection: What is the difference between rules and norms?
Rules are often imposed, norms are often decided by the group.

Ask students: What norms should we have for the course/semester?

Once students have made suggestions, place them on the board and together, decide on the 8-10 norms to be used for the course.

These should be revisited often and changed as needed.

Norms often include trust, safe spaces and respecting privacy, especially thinking about social media and those outside of class.

2. Timeline
(20-30 Minutes)

Ask students to create a timeline of their lives from birth until present and to highlight 3-5 major events that have shaped them as people, humans and Americans. They may also choose different identifiers that are meaningful (immigrant, person of color, etc.)

In identifying an event, they must also name a value that stems from the event and explain the connection between the value and event.

3. Museum of Me
(30-60 Minutes)

Ask students to bring in one item that belongs to them or a family heirloom that has been passed down and is meaningful. Ask students to label the items with a significant date, place of origin and a short description and to place the items around the room. Begin a silent gallery walk, followed up by a discussion on what values the objects represent and the value of telling our own histories. Students could also create an online gallery combining their timelines with their items and histories, allowing the work to remain for future classes.

4. Protest and Democracy
(30-45 minutes)

"Protest beyond the law is not departure from democracy; it is absolutely essential to it."-Howard Zinn

1. Pair share ideas of democracy as defined by students

2. Reactions to Howard Zinn quote

Point out to students the difference between a classical democracy and a representational one, where elected officials act on behalf of the citizens. Explain that people can influence the opinions of lawmakers by having their voices be heard through advocacy and voting. It might also be useful to have students research how democracy exists in different countries and/or cultures and how different people have come to define and critique democracy.

When students think about the quote, ask them to suggest instances where protest led to change, and ask them if they think the change was positive or negative.

1. What are historical examples of protests?

2. Who benefited from the protest and who did not?

3. What were the factors that made the protest successful or not?

4. Why would protest be essential to democracy?

5. Are there other factors that students can think of that are vital to democracy? If so, what are they and why are they crucial?

6. What are the drawbacks or challenges to living in a democracy?

7. Who benefits most/least from a democracy?

5. Thinking and Discussing Values
(45 minutes)

Have students choose three/multiple questions to reflect on for 15 minutes. In round 1, they find a partner and share responses. In round 2, they switch and listen to their partner. In round 3, they cross talk using guiding questions listed below. Students may also suggest their own discussion statement.

1. What is the difference between values, beliefs and opinion?
2. What surprised you about what your partner said?
3. What is one new take away from your discussion?

Questions for discussion:

1. Name a time when you felt silenced.
2. Why do you think one group might silence another?
3. How would you describe the word power? Name a time when you used your voice for power.
4. Is media neutral? Why or why not?
5. What should the role of education be?
6. Should schools teach activism?
7. What is the purpose of government?
8. Does democracy let everyone's voice be heard?
9. Why might adults misunderstand young people?
10. What role does the media play in democracy?
11. Should democracy be in every country in the world?
12. What is the greatest benefit of democracy?
13. What is a critique of democracy?
14. What are the consequences of using your voice?
15. What are the consequences of not using your voice?
16. Does being a leader always mean you have power?
17. Does being a follower mean you don't have power?
18. Activism is the way to progress. Agree or Disagree?

6. Character Study
(30-45 minutes)

Ask students to name a person that is working on some sort of change in society that they find impactful, interesting and/or inspiring.

Students usually think about "famous" heroes. Have them try to "localize" the learning by thinking about their schools, cities, families and their communities and neighborhoods. It might also be helpful to review a local newspaper or conduct a web search for individuals who are working on local issues. Readings from the suggested books in Chapter 3 can also be useful for providing examples.

1. What were the factors that influenced him/her to act?

2. What was this person's main cause or issue?

3. What do you think this person's legacy is?

4. What values drive/drove this person?

5. What challenges has this person faced or overcome?

6. What do you take away from learning about this individual?

7. Definition of An Activist
(20-30 minutes)

An individual who uses their mind, a medium and a message to communicate their values in order to improve society based on their worldview.

1. What would you change about this definition?

2. What are the strengths of this definition?

3. What are the limitations of this definition?

Ask students to suggest their own definition and share with group.

8. My Values Compass
(30-45 minutes)

Write down 30 (number can vary) different values on a laminated sheet. Cut out values and place in Ziploc bag for each student. Hand out to each student. (Consider coming up with the 30 values as a class and be sure to define the meaning of each value so all students are clear.)

Have students narrow down their values from 30 to top 12, then top 8, and ultimately, their top four values.

Each student will choose four top values to place on compass modeling each direction: North, South, East and West.

The north ("North Star") is the top value that students live their lives by.

1. What is your "North Star" value? Why?

2. How do you live your "North Star" value?

9. Desiderata
(45-60 minutes over multiple classes, at least 2-3)

Explain that Desiderata in Latin means desired things.

Ask students to read the poem silently. Ask them to underline passages or lines that speak to them.

Then read the poem together as a class, discussing each line and checking for understanding.

Ask students to write their own Desiderata poems.

While listening to their classmates, ask the students to see if they can identify the underlying values of each poem's author. Discuss.

10. Take A Stand
(30-45 minutes)

Students will explore personal opinions based on provocative statements by placing themselves along a physical spectrum:

Agree   Neutral   Disagree

Designate an area for each: Agree, Neutral and Disagree with degrees of variation in between.

Neutral means a student does not yet know enough about the topic to take a stand. They may also choose not to answer by abstaining a maximum of 3 times total during the exercise.

Every student will first choose where to stand, silently, based on their beliefs and opinions after each statement is read out loud.

Students should understand they must be ready to justify verbally, one at a time, where they are standing and why. Normally, the teacher is the one to select students to explain their position, but with developed trust and a safe environment, students may call on each other with the teacher listening. A variation is to have students pair share with partners and crosstalk about why and where they stand. It can add a level of complexity to have someone play devil's advocate.

It is vital that students feel both challenged to speak their truth and yet safe enough to disagree in a respectful way. It is beneficial to revisit class norms/rules before doing this exercise to ensure productive, safe and civil discourse.

Statements can be found on the following page. Statements are meant to be provocative and delineate a clear stance with various degrees of certainty. The list should reflect current events and incorporate international, national and local news and should be updated frequently.

Examples of provocative statements for Take A Stand:

Events suggested by students can be especially powerful, but may need to be reworded or edited for clarity and appropriateness before being called out to the group for movement and discussion. It would be wise to ask students for written suggestions first in order to assess. Every word in the statement matters and should be chosen carefully. Be mindful of bias and offer statements from multiple political views.

1. Young people can change society through social media.

2. Race is the most important factor in social mobility.

3. The American Dream is alive and well.

4. If I see someone harassing one of my peers, it is my responsibility to step in and stop it.

5. The Founding Fathers were racist.

6. The best way to make change is to vote.

7. Women should be paid as much as men.

8. The United States is a welcoming place for immigrants.

9. A friend of yours is cheating on a school assignment: you should definitely step in and let them know it is wrong.

10. Going to college is the best way out of poverty.

11. Climate change/global warming is real.

12. Activism should be taught in schools.

13. Service hours should be required in all schools.

5
THE BLUEPRINT: IMPARTING KNOWLEDGE

The blueprint serves as a guide for research, reflection and data gathering that will set students on a path to expertise and mastery of a subject or an issue. This is necessary so that their artifact-the product they will create based on the information researched-is as thorough and nuanced as possible. The blueprint evolves in a methodical, linear process of deep understanding and learning.

The blueprint is both intellectual and personal. It bridges the values portion of the course with a topic, cause or issue that the student has identified as connected to those values. The goal is to have the student feel that they are exploring their values through intellectual inquiry in way that is personal, intentional and thoughtful.

The blueprint is called impart because students are preparing to share the knowledge they have gathered with the world. They are becoming experts on their topic and are thinking about how best to align their passions and interests with a powerful message.

The intent behind this chapter is to provide a foundation that can be adapted by educators to their classrooms, curriculum and schools so that it yields the most powerful results for their students and communities.

It is imperative to allow plenty of time for students to conduct research that is thorough and complete. This might involve working with a librarian or media specialist and/or interviewing community members who work on the issue, topic or cause. In a 13 week course, at least 3-4 weeks should be allotted for the blueprint process.

The blueprint is both a document and process designed to help students break down a topic into questions that build on cumulative knowledge. Through the blueprint, the student should have the necessary information to create powerful artifacts that reflect their values, knowledge and voice. The ultimate goal is to create an effective message through the chosen medium. It may be shared as a paper copy or digitally.

The following questions should be followed in order as each question builds on what has come before. They are written speaking directly to the student.

REFLECT

1. What do you already know about your topic?

2. What do you wonder about your topic?

RESEARCH

3. What data (numbers/statistics, people and organizations) have you found on your topic and where did you find it? What bias and perspectives exist in your data? **Provide citations for all sources.**

RECORD

4. Summarize opinions about your topic from people both inside and outside of the school community. What values might drive their opinions? Which opinions are in contrast?

REASON

5. Why does your topic exist? Think about how the past has shaped the present.

6. Based on what you know so far, how do you predict your topic would change in the future? Why?

RECOLLECT

7. What do you think about your topic now, after having heard other opinions? Has your opinion changed? Why? If it has not changed, why not?

RESPOND

8. What is one action/solution to your topic that you think would solve or improve your topic?

9. What challenges would be posed by someone who disagrees with your solution? How would you respond to those challenges?

REVIEW

10. Why did you choose your topic? What value(s) drew you to your topic?

11. Do you think you've treated your topic fairly by considering both sides? Why or why not? What bias do you bring to your topic?

REACT WITH YOUR ARTIFACT

12. Taking a look at all of your information, what is the message you want to communicate about your topic? State the message using one sentence.

13. Who is your intended audience and what is the best medium in reaching that audience?

Questions 12 and 13 of the blueprint require careful consideration of the student's talents, skills and passions. For question 13, a menu of mediums (see page 12) must be chosen and presented to the students. Creating a podcast works well as a standard medium for all.

Students will require constant support through every section of the blueprint. It is extremely important that students provide citations for all sources. It is also useful to have students peer review their blueprints, as it often helps them catch oversights or errors and it can help them learn from seeing the work of others as examples.

It is vital that students learn to assess sources by relevance, quality and veracity in this age of "fake news." The best blueprints are the ones that understand both sides of an issue and can answer critiques in a full and honest way while relying on reliable sources and data.

It is highly recommended to first choose an issue as a class and have students complete the blueprint process together with teacher guidance. Different students can be in charge of different sections or the work can all be done together, question by question. The point is for students to learn the nuances of each section and be able to ask questions in a safe environment with no judgement.

Consider an example topic like homelessness to do together. It may be possible to combine this topic with actual service in a shelter and interviews with clients and staff in order to more deeply understand the roots and causes of the issue. One could pose an essential question around how and why homelessness happens.

Unfortunately, homelessness is a problem prevalent in almost every community within the country, and the issue is often forgotten or hidden. It is a topic that is familiar to students but has enough nuance depending on the city, population and societal and cultural context that it can serve as a solid topic for the blueprint process. Homelessness is affected by many different factors and involves humans that deserve attention, help and for their stories to be heard. It can also be a great foundation for incorporating service-learning.

There might be other issues that make sense to do as a class. One of the best ways to begin is to have students brainstorm issues they see as important within the community and develop short surveys that can be done in person or online to figure out what others think. Then the class can vote to figure out what topic will be chosen.

Once students have completed the blueprint, they are ready to take their topic and make it come alive through their chosen medium. They are ready to make art through their artifact. The data they have gathered through their blueprint has a clear, practical and powerful purpose-to educate and inspire their audience through an engaging message using the arts and technology. They are becoming creators.

6

THE ARTIFACT: PUT YOUR ART INTO IT

The third process in the Uncommon Civics continuum involves developing an artistic medium and a message built from the blueprint in order to develop voice. Artifacts combine art (medium) and data (blueprint) together into a powerful statement (message).

There are important pedagogical considerations when creating an artifact. Art is a powerful medium that can transcend identity and yet is affected by one's positioning in the world and viewpoints; it both shapes and is shaped by one's experience. One of the goals of the values and blueprint process is asking students to think about their own multiple identities and how they affect their worldview. It is vital that students feel like they can take calculated risks in their research and art in order to express themselves through their work.

The most crucial pedagogical shift is the ability for the student to move from spectator to creator. This is an important intellectual and emotional leap. Students receive countless messages each day on how and what to think. Advertisements and media never cease to speak. Social media has gained a large portion of societal attention, and so has the 24-hours news cycle. The reaction time to current events has been altered so there is little time to process the effects or contexts of information. Therefore, educators can strive to create for students the time and the space to process one issue, cause or topic at a time in a way that is thoughtful and reflective. The blueprint process facilitates a space for deep thought so that some of the noise can be filtered out and students can focus mindfully on a single issue.

A third focus for Uncommon Civics practitioners is to be inclusive of different learning styles, talents and passions. The mediums (listed on Pg. 12 and the next page) provide a wide menu of options to engage students with different learning needs and preferences and is therefore inclusive and student-centered.

An example will illustrate the point through the medium of posters. In her blueprint, this student explored how media frames the female body, specifically on magazine covers. She also struggled with her own issues of self-image, food and weight. She researched and created her own magazine cover. To the right of the model, she has included the words, "Your body was made for better things." This work forces us to engage with the image and consider what words like power, beauty and style mean in juxtaposition with a jarring image. The student has taken back the narrative on her own terms.

Using the artifact framework, the ST model outlined below can be helpful in directing students and creating assessments for the class.

The ST model for artifacts:

START: artifact creates a strong first impression on audience. The audience wants to know more and questions are raised about meaning and intent. The audience is pulled in and cannot look away.

STATISTICS: artifact uses numbers and data in creative ways. There is an appropriate balance so that numbers do not become confusing or overwhelm the medium. The numbers help deepen the story being told and increase the impact on the intended audience.

STORIES: artifact includes a narrative element that fosters connection, empathy and helps illustrate the impact of data on the population or community affected. The stories are presented in a way that is memorable and helps create a conversation through art.

STEPS: artifact contains concrete steps for a plan of action. There is something for the audience to do or a call to action and participation based on the information and viewpoint/opinion.

STATEMENT: artifact has a clear and potent message that is left with the audience. It can be a definitive statement or a question to consider, and the artifact encourages further and deeper reflection.

Menu of mediums used in the artifact component:

Theater, spoken word, comic books/graphic novels, speeches, monologues, photography, murals/street art, short films, including fiction and/or documentaries, posters, pamphlets, songs, podcasts and poetry. Other art forms are acceptable as long as they speak to the basic philosophy of the artifact: an artistic medium which helps communicate a message for action that is well researched, provocative and pushes boundaries.

The process of teaching through artifacts can be distilled to three steps: defining, aligning and designing:

Define: Students can identify their values and their origin in order to own the values that help them most make sense of their lives and become experts on their issue through the blueprint.

Align: students consider their values, the message from their blueprint and their intended audience in order to choose a medium that aligns all three and fits their talents, passions and interests.

Design: students create an artifact for their message through an artistic medium that fits their talents and intellectual interests, shifting from passive consumers to critical content and media creators.

When students already possess a particular talent with a specific medium, they should be encouraged to utilize those skills to focus more on the messaging and delivery. The Uncommon Civics course also serves as an opportunity for risk taking, especially for those students who do not think of themselves as being creative or artistic. Finally, students have the option of suggesting their own mediums.

The Uncommon Civics course teaches students the power to remix symbols, images and cultural narratives in a way that allows them to "talk back" to society in subversive, intelligent ways. This is what activists, media and advertising firms do. The message is everything. Images matter. Words matter. Mastering the message is the first step in creating change and learning to use voice from a place of confidence, creativity and strength.

One of the most powerful ways to connect the learning for students is to let them know the usefulness of turning the personal into the academic. Many students in the course have turned difficult, painful experiences of eating disorders, violence, heartbreak, relationship abuse and addictions into projects that were well researched, passionate and effective because they carried some pain and wisdom within the work. This work often helped with healing.

The Uncommon Civics process of unearthing values, developing the blueprint and creating artifacts helps students grow as both scholars and citizens. The focus of the handbook now shifts to systemic thinking on civic engagement for schools and communities.

7

THE CIVIC ENGAGEMENT MENU

Uncommon Civics is but one bright guiding star within a larger civic engagement universe. The last chapter focused on the student, the classroom and society. The next step is to take a bird's eye view of the field of civic engagement overall so that schools may choose how to engage with a clear understanding of associated terms under the umbrella term of civic engagement. The concepts addressed will be community service, service-learning, philanthropy/fundraising, advocacy/activism, social media and social entrepreneurship.`

It is important to differentiate these terms for two reasons. First, these terms are used often and sometimes interchangeably, which can lead to misalignment and unintended consequences. When the terms are confused, the work can be unclear. The second reason is that these terms have very different processes and outcomes, and they are underpinned by different values. Schools will choose programming based on mission, culture, resources and desired learning outcomes.

Even across different teaching and learning goals, there should always be an emphasis on clarity, intent and purpose. Students and communities deserve to have positive learning and service outcomes.

Definitions will be proposed with each term along with critical analysis always keeping in mind the goal of developing active citizens.

All concepts outlined serve important functions in developing civic engagement, and all have advantages and disadvantages in relation to the learning process and helping communities. Schools that understand these concepts can become stronger service partners.

Community service refers to kind acts that benefit both the doer and the recipient. They are acts that may provide temporary relief to pressing community needs that may be identified by the giver or the receiver.

Community service is important because it is often the first step a school undertakes towards civic engagement and can serve as a strong foundation for the other methods, especially service-learning. Therefore, it is wise to plan community service projects that lend themselves to possible connections to the curriculum.

The key to successful community service projects is in constantly thinking about context, collaboration and education. Communicating the reasoning of why a project was selected helps the community understand its importance to the school's mission and learning outcomes. Collaboration means working with the community partner to ensure the service rendered is timely, appropriate and useful. Educating the community helps explain a need or an issue on a deeper basis, therefore turning a service experience into opportunities for deeper reflection, learning and growth by expanding the community service into more complex forms of civic engagement.

Also important to note are the differences between charity and empathy. Charity seeks to provide relief, especially relevant in emergencies or tragedies that often require a very quick response because the need is great and urgent. Empathy involves projects that seek to understand the experience of those being served through connection, conversations and reflection. Both have their place in community service and it is helpful to consider the nuances of each.

Advantages: easy to plan and execute, feels great to help at some level, can be easily advertised for participation, instantly recognizable to most constituencies and can be organized with simpler logistics. Good for the image and soul of a school and/or community and great foundation for deeper civic engagement.

Disadvantages: can introduce or reinforce stereotypes if no learning context, can be mostly adult driven and there is often limited or no connection to curriculum or learning goals/targets.

Philanthropy/Fundraising is often well-meaning and seems simple enough: fundraise for a cause or issue through either collecting funds or selling some kind of product or service and donating the proceeds. These kinds of projects are good foundations for civic engagement as long as there is a consideration for some key questions:

1. Can all students donate? Is there any stigma for a student or community member that either cannot or chooses to not donate for financial or personal reasons?

2. Do students understand that fundraising is just one way to help a cause or solve a problem? Has there been a clear justification to the community about why fundraising is the best approach?

3. Did the students have a say in choosing the cause/project and the organizations where donations will be used? Has someone vetted the organization to know how the funds will be received? Are funds needed or would donating materials be a better use of time and money? Are there other resources that are needed more?

4. If an organization is national or international, can the students find a way to make a personal connection with staff and/or clients so they know how the funds will be used?

5. Can the giving be tied to a class project or piece of curriculum so the learning is enhanced?

Advantages: everyone can participate at different levels, makes school and/or community appear conscious, involved and generous and multiple causes can be helped at once. Can help build community and can be connected to learning projects with subjects like math and others depending on the cause. Can also be modified and evolved to service-learning.

Disadvantages: without proper context, it can send a wrong idea that only money solves problems. Can reinforce wealth and privilege and cause inequality to be magnified within a classroom, school or community.

Service-learning is the combining of service and learning goals to address community needs through a clear essential question.

Service-learning takes considerable time to plan and execute, and should include periodic reflection throughout all stages of the service: planning process, execution of the project and conclusion of project, including possible future steps. Throughout the process, teachers and students are grappling with a central question or theme so that it focuses the service and the learning. The service feeds the learning and the learning augments the service. There must exist a deeper contextualization process of why the service is needed and done.

There should be an emphasis on working on projects that are long-term, sustainable and build on reciprocal relationships.

The best service learning projects are planned and executed working with partner organizations so that learning targets are clearly aligned with the missions of the school and the partner organization.

Reflection, although often overlooked or rushed, is where much of the personal learning and growth occurs, and should occur often and be done in multiple ways, not simply saved for the end.

Advantages: can deepen learning for students and enhance applicability of subject matter, can lead to meaningful community connections and help learning and growth. When done well, service-learning can lead to new directions academically, professionally and personally for students. Service-learning can also help address critical needs in the community that would otherwise go unaddressed.

Disadvantages: can be challenging to plan logistically, congruence between curriculum and community needs can be difficult and community partners can feel overwhelmed with too many volunteers with different needs and expectations. Same concerns as community service with reinforcing stereotypes if there is not enough work on historical, cultural and political context. Finally, concepts around power, voice and agency may arise and it requires faculty feel equipped and be properly trained and supported to lead difficult conversations with students, community partners and parents.

Advocacy/Activism is where the Uncommon Civics class lives and it can be extended to other realms like social media, social entrepreneurship and service-learning. As a pedagogy, it is strongest when students have a solid foundation in the facts surrounding an issue or a problem, a thorough understanding of arguments against their particular opinion, a solid grounding in the historical, political and cultural contexts of the issues, and real world experience with those individuals or organizations already working on the issue.

As long as the process is tied to learning in the classroom; activism and advocacy are conducted in a peaceful and respectful way of laws (as long as those laws are consistent with basic human and civil rights); and students have largely been responsible for their own opinions, learning and political stances, schools should encourage advocacy and activism as a way to apply learning to the real world.

There are different levels of comfort with values based discussions and political leanings within schools and communities, but remaining neutral is impossible. These leanings exist within the curriculum, both implicitly and explicitly. Schools should not teach students what to think but instead how to identify a perspective and bias, how to recognize one's own perspective and its limits and how to form a critical argument that speaks to one's own values and the actual issue being discussed. This is the process of preparing students to live their values and be able to receive and respond to critique and different, even opposite views. Schools can serve as crucial laboratories for democratic debate and dialogue.

Schools must also figure out a way to reflect current events while at the same time placing the present within past and future narratives. Context and multiple perspectives are what facilitate learning and growth for a community, a classroom and a democracy.

Advantages: students enjoy spaces where they can develop as political beings with support from peers and adults, they can try out political stances with relative safety and schools can become living laboratories for civic and civil discourse.

Disadvantages: can be perceived as indoctrination if not done or presented correctly, difficult to find time and space for teaching within school day and schedule and requires sustained support and professional development for faculty as new societal issues emerge.

Social Media is a cultural phenomenon and tool/outlet that few schools and institutions have been prepared to handle and much less teach. It falls under civic engagement because it is so crucial to understanding the cultural zeitgeist. It is an indispensable tool for students to understand and learn how to use. This also means understanding how serious and dangerous social media can be if handled poorly.

While there might be school policies around responsible use, there are few schools preparing students to be adept at managing both their online presence and their messaging. There is also the challenge of knowing that as soon as one type of social media is discussed, a new medium or technology will be unveiled.

Nevertheless, it is important to persist because media is being thrown at students at an alarming rate and they must have a way to process, discern and speak back to an incredible amount of information. They must also be able to tell what is real and what is propaganda. There is also the question of "slacktivism." If a student finds a cause engaging online, they should have additional outlets to explore said cause in an academic setting. It is not enough to simply click away with no further learning, context or conversation.

Educators can look to past examples of social media and use those as case studies to probe further. There are plenty of examples to pull from: KONY 2012, Ice Bucket Challenge, #metoo movement, #neveragain, #fakenews, etc.

All of them will have unique characteristics, but it is worthwhile to develop a general framework of questions for students to explore in class and for administrators to consider on a school wide level.

If teaching the Uncommon Civics class, this is a discussion best introduced when the blueprint is done and students are finishing with their artifacts. If the artifact lends itself to social media messaging, this is a crucial conversation before the artifact is completed.

Educators should be proactive in thinking about how social media affects the everyday reality of students and what is being taught in the classroom. On the following page are some guiding questions to begin thinking about social media and the learning process.

The questions can be expanded to include any social media medium/platform:

1. What does it mean when something goes viral?
2. What parts of your life should be public and which ones should be private?
3. What online persona or presence do you have?
4. What social media platforms have you (or would you) choose to represent your life? Do you use different platforms for different audiences?
5. Would you choose a different platform to represent your political views? Why or why not?
6. What messages do you think you'd want to communicate based on your values and opinions? What hashtags would you use? Why?
7. How will you discern what is true and factual?
8. Who is included in your message? Who is left out?
9. What could be consequences (positive and negative) of you voicing your opinion?
10. How will you handle those who disagree with your message or stance?

Social media is filled with peril but also potential. The whole wide world and web is watching, judging and never forgetting.

Advantages: The right message can quickly reach thousands or millions of users, multiple social media outlets for different messaging, talents and audiences. Movements can be created from a smartphone.

Disadvantages: A message can quickly spiral out of control, social media can expose an individual or institution to embarrassment, legal action, bullying or violence. Prevalence of incorrect or fake information makes it difficult to discern what is true and real. Social media conversations may also present free speech challenges and blur the lines between personal and professional perspectives.

Social Entrepreneurship can help engage students who have an interest or talent for combining business and service. Through social entrepreneurship, students brainstorm a business plan with a product or service that may have two bottom lines: being profitable and helping the community. Put another way, its value is not just based on how much the business venture makes, but how much it helps. The power of this civic engagement method is that it can pull from so many different disciplines at once: design thinking, economics, ethnographies, sociology and marketing/advertising. It can be a very useful model for planning projects "with" communities as opposed to "for" and lends itself to project based learning and can be a great extension of existing service-learning projects.

Social entrepreneurship also sends an important message to students that it is not necessary to divide one's life and professional goals between "doing good" and "doing well." It is possible to have ideas, create products and start companies that do both. It is also vital that students understand that for-profit entities can also be concerned with their impact on society and can actively look for ways to give back to the community. The concept of doing good and doing well can live in any organization, school or company, as long as their values, mission and actions aim for service to a community.

Advantages: Can engage individuals with entrepreneurial mindsets and can serve as strong links between business classes and communities in need with innovative service.

Disadvantages: Can lead to low impact service projects and service focus can suffer or shift if profit margins change.

8

LEADING SERVICE AND LEARNING

The role of the civic engagement professional varies across education sectors within higher education, K-12, public or private institutions, all with differing missions. There are different mandates, budgets, schedules and classes and the work reaches across multiple areas of need. Many schools enact civic engagement through an administrator, some charge teachers with the specific role of leading service-learning for certain grades and others rely on teachers to implement their own projects only within their classrooms. Some schools do not have any sort of position deepening the public mission of the institution and may only rely on charity.

The goal of this chapter is to begin forming a cohesive narrative highlighting, celebrating and perhaps even defending this role. Every school in our nation, and even our world, should enable a person with the position, influence and power to craft and lead civic engagement initiatives. The goal of this chapter is to elucidate what roles, functions and dispositions the civic professional should understand and fulfill. This should be useful to current practitioners, teachers looking to move into administration and hiring committees.

The functions of an individual leading service and learning fall into three categories: a civic engagement philosophy; the community and school spheres; and the seven realms of civic engagement for civic engagement professionals-learning, teaching, service, leadership, management, and student and program development.

A powerful way to begin thinking about civic engagement is to create a service philosophy statement underpinning the values around how a school understands their civic responsibilities. Creating a service statement can help turn a school mission statement into concrete outcomes that can be executed, assessed and improved upon. Here is mine as an example to consider and critique:

1. Service is centered and grounded around the school mission and values. Schools must designate individuals, resources, and support to carry out service-learning based on the school's mission, values and communities.

2. There is an important difference between community service, service-learning, fundraising/philanthropy, activism/advocacy, social media and social entrepreneurship. All are part of a civic engagement menu and schools can have different specialties and foci, as long as they know that all have different learning outcomes. At the very least, schools should have a community service program as a foundation.

3. Service-learning is developed around foundational central questions or themes that drive and direct the learning, with clear and specific curricular connections.

4. Service-learning uses reflection throughout the process, not just the end, and it is done in ways that engage all students.

5. Service-learning works to enhance assets, strengths and gifts on both sides of the partnership.

6. Effective service learning first asks questions of the community, listens and works to address their concerns.

7. Service-learning asks difficult questions around power, privilege, voice, inclusion and justice and creates environments where these questions can be discussed for the sake of deeper learning.

8. Service-learning considers the historical, social, political, economic and cultural context of the communities doing the service and those served.

9. High-quality professional development is provided to educators practicing service-learning, especially at the K-12 level.

10. Service-learning can serve as a bridge between private and public institutions through mutually beneficial partnerships.

What would your tenets be and why?

Along with a foundational statement, a civic engagement pedagogy can help guide and shape ideas to deepen learning.

The following five pedagogical principles of civic engagement can serve as guides for program development to ensure positive outcomes for both students and communities and promote best practices for the field of civic engagement.

Consider a learning goal with a need in the community and see how well it meets the following criteria for service and learning:

1. *Essential question:* This is a question that is clear, concise and will drive the learning for the duration of the project. They are central to the curriculum and to the service. The questions serve as an anchor for the service and an engine for the learning. For example, the essential question for the Uncommon Civics course is "What makes a good citizen"? Every activity, reading, field experience and project helps to answer this question. The best service and learning projects have a provocative, challenging and relevant essential question that is both open-ended and can be answered. It connects the classroom to the community and centers the learning for students and partners.

2. *Reciprocal partnerships:* There is an exchange between the school and the community through partnerships, and both parties avoid deficit thinking. Instead, there is a focus on finding assets on both sides and the best ways to meaningfully share those assets.

3. *Context:* The "why" of a project, and the surrounding questions around why a need exists are taken seriously and are central parts of the curriculum. Context is derived and created from speaking with clients, staff and communities involved in the partnership and augmented with research, readings, reflection and class discussions. Cultural, historical and political contexts increase relevance and help establish conversations around power, inclusion, voice and justice.

4. *Meaning:* There is sustained reflection at the beginning, middle and end of the service and learning experience that moves beyond "me." There is a focus on what the experience might mean for others and a focus on growth and building empathy beyond the individual.

5. *Voice and story:* Conversations are created, sustained and celebrated through service and learning. Multiple forms of reflection are offered throughout the service experience with a particular focus on the power of connection, storytelling, witnessing and recording.

Now, a deeper discussion on the community and school realms.

The community sphere:

Community Partners: Community partners are the foundation for all civic engagement; they are essential to good work. The ability to assess whether an organization would make a good partner rests on the ability to discern certain qualities through thoughtful questions and active, careful listening. The importance of a site visit cannot be overstated; a site visit before any service occurs is fundamental.

This is why it is recommended crafting a civic engagement philosophy as an initial step to help guide the visit and conversations and highlighting the "fit" with a potential partner. Likewise, it is crucial the partner also determine if the school is a good fit for the project. It is a conversation and reflection that must run both ways.

Questions that can help establish a good partnership:

1. Does the organization seem to understand the difference between community service and service-learning?
2. Where does the organization need the most help and is the school/classroom equipped to be able to help those needs?
3. Is there a point person dedicated to fostering partnerships with schools or within the community?
4. Does the school, class schedule and transportation plan work with the hours, work and mission of the organization?
5. Is there a dedicated budget on school side to support the project and if not, is there a plan for fundraising funds or collecting material donations?
6. Is the organization willing to teach along with being a place to serve? Is there staff dedicated to translating the service into contextual, deep learning?

A civic engagement professional has to be as comfortable walking into a scrappy non-profit run by a shoestring budget and miracles as they are meeting with a national board and CEO. They must understand the pressures of a non-profit and the intricacies of what it takes to run a mission-based organization that can differ greatly from schools, along with its unique terminology, times of stress and different notions of learning and civic engagement. Understanding what partners organizations need is key to crafting powerful projects.

The school sphere:

Individuals in these positions must have their finger on the pulse of the school, from the first grade taught to the school leadership. There should be a consideration for having this person report directly to the leader of the school. There should be appropriate funding for the program with adequate administrative support.

The most important question a director can ask within a community is "How is this person/constituency affected by civic engagement?" From there, multiple questions emerge:

1. What does civic engagement mean to this individual?
2. Why should they care about civic engagement?
3. What is the best way to engage with this person/constituency in a way that honors where they are in their learning process?

Now the seven realms of leading service learning:

Learning:

This person should be well-versed in the current research around service-learning and the historical evolution of service within schools. They should also have a clear theory on how learning happens and a solid educational philosophy with values that align with the school and its mission. This person also needs to be an expert or near-expert in curriculum development. They need to be able to look at unit, semester or year-long plans of instruction and see spaces where service-learning can live or where other forms of civic engagement are appropriate. They need to understand the science of learning and how the brain retains information, especially through reflection and experiential learning. They should also have some understanding of learning styles and differences to adapt activities as necessary.

Teaching:

Skills in presenting to faculty, students and community partners with appropriate language that is clear, concise and positive. They should strive to teach at least one course where they can practice what they teach through a service-learning course.

Service:

It is crucial to create a working definition of service-learning in relation to community service. These two concepts are often the foundation for civic engagement in schools. Clear definitions can be helpful if there is a school/graduation requirement. Directors should strive to practice meaningful service with students and in their own lives for a cause or issue so as to model for the school community.

Leadership:

Civic engagement leaders must find ways to be part of the leadership conversations within the school and be able to suggest policies that are in line with the civic mission and vision of the school. They should be part of professional networks around character education, civic engagement and service-learning for student development. They should be active contributors to the field of civic engagement by writing articles, attending and presenting at conferences and seizing opportunities to shape policy and thought.

Management:

Directors should have a clear grasp on budgeting and advocating for funding of their program and its particular needs. It also helps to have a policy on how fundraising will be handled for any partnerships or causes. The ability to write and assess grants is useful, along with marketing expertise for varies constituencies. They must also have a deep understanding of logistics and scheduling, knowing how to move a large number of people safely and effectively to service sites and using time effectively. This person also needs to have a grasp on messaging and marketing for crafting powerful and cohesive narratives about service that are rooted in the mission. This means creating language that varies depending on the constituencies engaged and being able to celebrate and highlight different voices to include students, faculty, administrators, community partners, clients served and other civic engagement professionals. They must know how to look for quality in learning outcomes in vendors. Finally, they must have an ability to discern program areas in need of improvement and the support and training to address deficiencies.

Program Development:

There are countless acronyms designed to help educators craft powerful civic engagement initiatives. Many often resemble a similar structure: identify a need, research a need, serve, reflect on the service and celebrate. While general models can be useful, good program development is a unique process that will yield different outcomes, models and procedures because every school and community is unique. The challenge is for schools to develop models that fit their mission, values and goals for each student/graduate and community member. That said, it is important to note certain parameters that can be useful for current/future civic education leaders.

One must have a firm grasp of how reflection, listening, power, voice and agency interact and conflict at all steps of planning a project. Developing empathy as opposed to sympathy for all parties involved (community partners, students, teachers, clients, parents, etc.) and being able to see how a project might be accessed and perceived by each constituency is crucial to every project.

Just as important as a firm grasp on logistics is the ability to discern risk and to mitigate dangers of threats, both in the sense of keeping volunteers physically safe but also with a concern for psychological and emotional safety for the communities served. This kind of work involves focusing specifically on power, voice and agency, and it is vital to keep in mind as the planning progresses because it is easy to be overwhelmed by logistics and learning goals.

The ability and power to transcend models of how adults have been taught enables educators to imagine new possibilities for effective program development. Outdated pedagogies that no longer explain our rapidly changing society must be reimagined. This question seems particularly important in civics, but it pervades across all subjects and disciplines. High quality civic engagement does not live in isolation from other subjects or only in the Uncommon Civics classroom; it borrows from and is strengthened by having multiple disciplines speak to an issue or cause in collaboration.

Last, there is an aim to have programs where students identify not only their cause, but their because. They figure out not only what they care about, but why they care about it. They find deeper purpose in their work because what they are learning has real connections to what they see around them. Students feel challenged and empowered.

Student Development:

The ultimate goal of civic engagement is to see the student grow and develop as both a scholar and a citizen. This requires having a clear vision and understanding of the scope and limits of the program. Many different ideas and suggestions come across the desk of a civic engagement professional. A good number of ideas come from students, and sometimes ideas are suggested by parents or community members. One of the more interesting facets of this job is that ideas are often deeply tied to passions and commitments, and so ideas can be intellectual and emotional in nature. However, not every good idea makes for a good service project.

One of the most difficult, yet necessary skills to have as a civic engagement professional and especially an educator is to be able to discern the doable from the impossible. There are projects that cannot be executed because they are not within the scope of the program, use up an unreasonable amount of resources, such as time, money or talent, or there are important and real safety concerns that go beyond stereotypes. The method to begin addressing these varied requests is to begin with a solid foundation of one's own values and their alignment with the institution, and follow or craft a civic engagement statement that reflects those values. It then becomes easier to make judgement calls when an idea is offered. Oftentimes, students suggest ideas and it is assumed the educator will help make it happen, but it must be a partnership between the educator and the student. The options to support, edit or rescind an idea is a skill that can lead to much higher quality programs with depth over breadth.

A secondary focus of student development is preparing the student for challenges and possibly failure. Some service projects will fail even after committing considerable time and effort. Some factors are beyond control. The question is how to best respond to failure.

Finally, the idea of civic engagement beyond schooling is vital. How can students take their service ideas, passions and projects and align them with future opportunities? How can the next generation of civic engagement professionals be supported? The answer to these questions will ultimately shape our society and world. It is imperative to consider how schools can improve the framing and teaching of civic engagement and how to best equip professionals to do good work for society, for communities, and ultimately, for every student.

CONCLUSION: AN UNCOMMON VISION

Uncommon Civics speaks directly to the dual role of every school, no matter the specific mission or focus: to build scholars and citizens. As educators, both roles are fulfilled by developing student voice.

The tagline for Uncommon Civics as a movement is "Become the change you speak." The idea of voice is so fundamental to what educators do and what democracy requires that it deserves a central place within the curriculum, the classroom and the country.

There is need for a new sort of skillset around citizenship as outlined in this book that moves beyond "how a bill becomes a law."

The notion that civic engagement in our schools is optional can no longer be accepted. This is a time full of cynicism, tribalism, hyper awareness of news, mistrust in public institutions and a lack of respect for truth, all which threaten not only our civic discourse, but also our existence as a nation. Civics is not just about laws, dates and citizenship exams, it is about the very heart and soul of America, they are the ideals the country is based on and the values that are presented as American. Although this book was conceptualized in America, the lessons and teachings within this book can be applied wherever civic engagement for youth is valued, needed or threatened.

This book was written with a deep respect for students and educators. Although there are multiple institutions responsible for building citizens, none have the initial impact of schools on young people. This is what makes the work of teachers and educators so vital, challenging and important. Their wisdom is desperately needed.

The Uncommon Civics course was originally taught to juniors as a required course under a different name. The following anecdote highlights the power and potential of the class for young people.

One of my students became interested in a photography project highlighting the lived realities of Native Americans, and so she researched photography highlighting societal inequality, and came across photographers documenting the Native American experience. She happened to come across the work of Aaron Huey and his TED talk on work done with the Lakota Sioux in Pine Ridge, South Dakota. The light switch was turned on. Through her blueprint, she focused on the inhumane conditions present in the Pine Ridge Reservation. Her chosen topic spoke to her need for seeking justice. History had come alive. Her work was not just about a grade, but about combining her talents to serve a greater cause. She finished her blueprint and began creating a spoken-word poem in podcast form entitled "Nightwolf." In it, she imagines from a first person perspective what it must have been like to be Lakota throughout history. The student was able to use her knowledge of history, theatre and narrative to create a breathtaking and heartbreaking art piece.

This student learned to use her voice through raising awareness of an issue that was important to her and important to society. She first researched an artist that exemplified the power of witnessing through his photography with a deep respect for Lakota culture and community. The student took great care to show empathy in her podcast while moving beyond sympathy or pity. She became a media creator and the work was so powerful and well-crafted that one was forced to listen. The audience cannot look away and must engage.

The student went on to research other ways to help and came across Re-Member (www.re-member.org), and with support from adults, helped organize and lead a life-changing service-learning trip to Pine Ridge, therefore benefitting other students. This student is a great example of how to be uncommon in witnessing with heart.

What is done in classrooms shapes what kind of society and world exist. The hope within this book is to create communities where individuals are constantly tying their acts of kindness, volunteering and activism to their "why." When individuals in a society can articulate their values and passion for certain causes, it inspires others to do the same. Schools can be places where the value and power of voice is first taught to students as they become citizens.

This idea of risk taking is the very soul of citizenship and the aim of Uncommon Civics: to create citizens that are willing to take chances and calculated risks for what they believe in for a more just society. The story of America is a story of individuals standing up for their ideals. The story of activism across history is people standing up for their beliefs despite the risks, dangers and consequences.

Schools that ignore developing civic intelligence and citizenship for the sake of other priorities, trends or skills risk turning out smart individuals with little idea how to apply their knowledge beyond themselves. There must be more to life than just personal gain.

In contrast, schools that are adept and advanced in service and learning have more opportunities to develop civic intelligence. Schools that have created academic spaces for classes like Uncommon Civics will have students who are better equipped to ask and answer "why" questions. Adults who are trained in teaching Uncommon Civics and have lived lives of purpose and active volunteering will be better equipped to support and model for students what it means to live a life of civic engagement. Schools that have supported learning spaces for classes like Uncommon Civics have set students up for success because students will know their civic purpose. These students are ready to be uncommon citizens.

There is a need for constructive disagreement, even for what has been written in this book. Democracy is ultimately about arguments-not bickering or conflict for the sake of ego-but competing visions of what America is and what it can be. Good civic engagement is about teaching students how to create the most powerful arguments possible and listening deeply to dissenting viewpoints and opinions.

This book was written with a deep love and appreciation for this country's promise. Through its lessons, democracy can thrive. The imperfections of institutions can be made more perfect. Needs can be met through service projects that speak to the humanity and goodness of humankind while not ignoring the systems that work to oppress, silence and disappear voices. A better world can be created where young people constantly work for improving our society through using their voice and moving from message to action. There can be more nuanced narratives from silenced voices that go beyond statistics and headlines. Students can grow as citizens, artists and scholars. Young people, with the right support, can be uncommon in making their voices heard through civics, art and service for learning.

ABOUT THE AUTHOR

Diego Iván Durán-Medina was born in Caracas, Venezuela. He graduated from Colgate University, New York University and Columbia University-Teachers College. He has worked as a teacher, administrator and consultant in Washington, D.C., New York City, Hawaii, Colorado and Florida.
He is the author of multiple articles on service-learning and civic engagement. He founded LeadServe Consulting in 2013 to help schools become better at developing both scholars and citizens.
Since 2015, he has served as Director of Service-Learning at Shorecrest Preparatory School in St. Petersburg, Florida. In 2017, he co-founded the Center for Service Learning Leadership (CSLL) dedicated to helping independent school educators create and improve service projects tied to classroom learning. More information can be found at www.leadingservicelearning.org and www.leadserveconsulting.com.
In 2018, he founded Uncommon Civics, a pedagogy and movement dedicated to improving the teaching of civics and developing better citizens.

Made in the USA
Middletown, DE
19 April 2022